To Judge John,

In sincere gratitude
for your years of leader-
ship at Wornall Road
and for your many
kindnesses to me.

R. Lofton Hudson

TAPROOTS FOR **TALL** SOULS

Author of

The Religion of a Sound Mind

and

The Religion of a Mature Person

R. Lofton Hudson

TAPROOTS FOR

Tall

SOULS

BROADMAN PRESS • NASHVILLE, TENNESSEE

Printed in the United States of America
7.5F54RRD.

DEDICATED

TO

Patricia Ann Hudson
My Growing Eight-Year-Old

FOREWORD

I AM happy in the privilege of introducing what I know you will consider a delightful study. I have known the author since his early student days. He has honored me with his confidence in times of important decisions, and I have been with him in all his pastorates except the present one. I published his first book, and have read with interest and profit the galleys of this new one.

This thoughtful volume is written specifically to aid those who are trying to grow spiritually. Dr. Hudson does not permit his knowledge of philosophy and psychiatry and his acquaintance with technical terms to keep him from presenting in forceful and everyday language the great truth that the secrets of spiritual growth are in God's Word.

I like the truth of this sentence, "We count Christians when we ought to measure them." This book would make Christians count. Naturally the chapters will have special appeal to different readers. I like especially those dealing with "The Man in the Basement" (instinctual life) and "The Man Upstairs" (conscience). Possibly the strongest chapter is the one on "Taproots for Tall Souls."

Other chapters stress "The Growing Kind," "Getting Along with People," "Praying Right," "Real Food for Growth," and "Consider the Lilies." In this last named the author shows what to do when the brakes do not work or the clutch is slipping. The closing chapter, "Keep Moving!" shows how to be strong in the Lord. You will like this volume.

JOHN L. HILL

PREFACE

DR. LEON SAUL writes that "within every grown-up lives the little child he once was." And Dr. Edmund Bergler says, "Neurotics are never as old as their birth certificate shows them to be"—meaning that they often regress to an earlier stage of development.

I do not like the word "neurotic" because it means so many different things to different people. The time was when people said, "Thou fool"; now they say, "Thou neurotic." But labels are deceptive and unfair. Who is not a little neurotic at times, if he is worth his salt? At least it may be said, to paraphrase Bergler, that no Christian is as mature as he ought to be.

So many people whom I know have a great and persistent desire to grow. It is one of man's basic needs. Often they simply do not know what to do. "How can I grow?" is often heard. One (physically) grown person said to me, "I have decided to grow up." She did not know how "growing pains" hurt, but her decision was a good one.

This book is aimed at helping just such people. The essays are frankly addressed to the reader. What book is not, for that matter? If they sound like spoken words, this is because the author is so accustomed to speaking. They are not sermons. At least, they were not all preached from a pulpit. That some of the material was used in the author's own preaching is gladly admitted. The important point is, that they are an attempt to aid those who are trying to grow spiritually. If they accomplish that purpose, a worthy goal will have been achieved.

CONTENTS

Foreword by John L. Hill...................... vii

Preface ix

I. Grow Up or Blow Up......................... 1

II. Are You the Growing Kind?.................... 14

III. The Man in the Basement...................... 22

IV. The Man Upstairs............................. 37

V. Taproots for Tall Souls........................ 51

VI. Learning to Manage Myself.................... 61

VII. Growth in Getting Along with People............ 74

VIII. You'll Grow If You Pray Right.................. 89

IX. Real Food for Growth........................103

X. Consider the Lilies How They Grow............117

XI. Keep Moving! 131

No, when the fight begins within himself,
A man's worth something. God stoops o'er his head,
Satan looks up between his feet—both tug—
He's left, himself, i' the middle: the soul wakes
And grows. Prolong that battle through his life!
Never leave growing till the life to come!
                              "Bishop Blougram's Apology"

Put alongside these, two statements by contemporary prose writers, and you have the churches' greatest challenge and man's greatest need clearly before you.

The first comes from the pen of a Harvard psychiatrist, Dr. Robert W. White, in a recent book called *Lives in Progress:* [1]

Now that man has become so troubled about himself, so alarmed at his ineptitude in organizing a social system to suit the small world created by modern communication and modern scientific discoveries, he urgently needs to know more about his own potentiality for constructive growth. . . . He deserves a picture of himself that will not omit the highly human qualities of trying to understand things and change them for the better. . . . The natural growth of personality and the higher flights of human achievement have been given almost no representation in man's current ideas about himself.

The other quotation is from an "advice" columnist whom most of us have read in our daily newspapers, Angelo Patri. He says: [2]

You know now that maturity did not come like a birthday gift, neatly tied and wrapped and tagged. It came along in driblets, so tiny as to be invisible to the eye of watchful guardians and eagle-eyed lawmakers. It came in the night, stealthily and in the bright light of day in riotous sport. It came in hours of painful labor, in periods of unhappy restlessness. Always it was signed in by your eager, quivering, young self that strained at its bonds of childishness.

What Angelo Patri says of the young is also true of the old. All of us find ourselves straining at "the bonds of childishness."

GROW UP OR BLOW UP

POETS have tried to show us what we may become. Their method is a simple one. They point to something near by and say, "Be like that." In ancient Israel it was the dank, green, tough cedar. "He shall grow like a cedar in Lebanon," the psalmist sang out, speaking of one of God's people (Psalm 92:12). Good enough for the inside of Solomon's Temple. Fragrant enough for the most beautiful sanctuary then known. Enduring and stout enough for beams to support the heavy roof of God's house. The reference was not to the speed with which cedars grow, for actually they grow very slowly. Else the figure would have been false, for human growth is always very slow.

Lowell preached the same sermon: "Build thee more stately mansions, O my soul." Years had lapsed, but human hearts had not changed. It was a necessary note to be sounded. Edwin Markham likened us to a tree resisting a storm, which must send down deep roots on the windward side in order to strengthen itself.

It was always growth in conflict, moving on in a tragic state of tension. But the tension is more tragic to those who try to stand still. Browning put it this way:

Our Real Danger

It is customary these days to try to frighten ourselves by the buggerbear of atomic and hydrogen bombs. I, for one, do not know what to believe about how critical our situation really is. When the atomic scientists invent bombs which are so powerful that they advise the governments not to use them, I begin to feel some alarm. In fact, scientists like Dr. Harold C. Urey, who know the real danger and warn against another world conflagration, could frighten me out of my wits if I did not have faith in God. It seems that our world possesses instruments of destruction which are too dangerous for children like ourselves to play with.

Dr. Frank C. Laubach, in a very thought-provoking book entitled *Wake Up or Blow Up,* has offered a solution to our seeming crisis. He says, among other important things, that "you can't win a cold war with hot weapons." As far as I am concerned he is both right and wrong. He is probably wrong in implying that we cannot deter Communist aggression by military means. His error might even be a suicidal one for democracy. But he is right in contending strenuously for the need for material aid and for Christian missionaries as a means of combating Red ideas which are carefully planted by zealous Communist emissaries. He is keenly aware of the peril of our world and not too optimistic, it seems to me. Perhaps he knows enough to have his fears well grounded.

On the other hand, fears may be largely the projection of our own natural insecurity. Most of the time I feel that straining our eyes at the horizon in expectation of some Armageddon is a distraction from our real problems. Destruction *may* come, but there are other things, like age and death, which will certainly come. Perhaps we had better spend our time on matters which will be of some avail if—or until—destruction comes and will certainly be of primary importance if the world rocks along very much as in the past.

Individually and as societies, it is possible to "blow up" without any great noise or without radioactive materials.

Korea has been a center of moral failure regardless of whether the atomic bomb has been, or will ever be, transported to its shores. South Africa will explode, one way or another, unless races learn to live together as adults. Europe seems to be sitting on a powder keg. And who knows where the next social, economic, or historical outrage will appear?

But are these our real problems? Are they not the expression of multiplied millions of voices which have rallied to the wrong slogans and followed the wrong Pied Piper?

For most of us the areas of our own arrested development are manifested much closer to home. Home—there is displayed our grossest infantilism. Next would probably be the market place, the office, the store, the factory, or the farm. Then follow closely the failures at school and in community activities. "The lonely crowd," to use the book title of a current sociologist, has become lonely because the individual members are trying to live in a false world under the leadership of false gods.

Danger to the Churches

Even in the churches we see all sorts of evidences of immaturity. If the communion is not one of considerable authoritarianism, we have "splits," "squabbles," and "cut-throat competition." If doctrines and practices are enforced by threat of damnation or appeals to nursery motives, there exist blind obedience, childish reasoning, and the most puerile sort of compulsive (ritualistic) behavior. It was Emerson who said that "everything God has made has a crack in it." Many church people are very frank, though apologetic, about applying Emerson's dictum to the church.

The word "crack," though graphic, is misleading. Cracks do not close up usually except by pressure from outside. The center of our human problems, many modern thinkers feel, is in the heart. Which is another way of saying that the solutions to human problems are not mechanical or statistical but personal and communal. People must grow, in other words, if they are to avoid catastrophe, personally or collectively.

It seems that there is an increasing number of people in the world who wish, with George Eliot,

> To make undying music in the world,
> Breathing a beauteous order that controls
> With growing sway the growing life of man.
>
> *The Choir Invisible*

What a blessing it would be if these who are interested could communicate with each other and, by the grace of God, find the way out. To say that people need to be saved does not seem to be a very profound remark any more. Most observing people will admit that. But that human, spiritual growth is a part of this saving process seems to be the point at which many hesitate. And to find the means of growth is even more crucial. At least, that is the approach of this discussion, and I doubt that anyone will be inclined to reject it, as far as it goes.

The churches of Jesus Christ have a real stake in human growth. Buildings, organizations, programs, worship services, evangelizing techniques, and every other religious exercise aim at one goal: the growth of individuals. They are not so much interested in conformity or group-spirit or obedience— or, for that matter, individual initiative—except as these are a part of each person's inner response to God and to divine goals. It is self-realization under God that is our primary objective.

Of course, we are not the only ones in our culture who are interested in growth. The schools are necessarily concerned. The home, at its best, is constantly working to grow the child into an adult. Mental health leaders, including psychiatrists especially, are thinking in terms of growth. All psychotherapists know that the prevention and cure of mental illnesses involves a very important kind of growth. We might say that everyone who is seriously and intelligently interested in people, rather than things and ways of life, is aware that human growth is *the* human problem.

But how does the church's approach to this problem differ from others? Are the churches concerned for intellectual and social growth as the schools are? Many parents give most of their thought to physical growth (health) and to getting the child ready for earning a livelihood.

Psychologists Look at Growth

Take the aims of psychology as an example. The noted psychoanalyst, Dr. Karen Horney, says that the broad aim of psychoanalytic therapy "includes change from compulsiveness to freedom and self-direction, from inertia to spontaneity, from indiscriminate hostility to active and discriminate friendship, from self-neglect to interest in self-development, and from a sense of isolation to real independence and joy in living and working with others." [3] Viewed from the standpoint of human research alone, this is a very comprehensive goal. The church can give enthusiastic approval to this aim, as far as it goes.

Christians, however, would ask the psychologists some very important questions. What is the direction of this freedom and spontaneity? How does man know where to direct himself? And to whom is this discriminate friendship to be directed?

Likewise, hostility? Is the individual to understand that he needs no guidance but his own reason and the social mores in expressing friendship or hostility? Does he need no power but his own inner resources in overcoming hate? And how can wounds caused by self-neglect be healed except by someone who can give unconditional love? (Who can do that, except God?) Furthermore, is "real independence" what man seeks? Or is it interdependence?

Gordon W. Allport of Harvard has given a very understandable and somewhat comprehensive criteria for maturity. It involves three main points: [4]

First, a grown person is one who "can lose himself in work, in contemplation, in recreation, and in loyalty to others." Second, he must have "that peculiar detachment from self" which is involved in a "sense of humor." Third, if he is mature, he will have developed "a unifying philosophy of life." Few will question that mature people have at least these three qualities and live in such a way that all three are demonstrated.

But this standard of maturity will not satisfy the Christian. Do not the Communist, the gangster, and the traitor "lose" themselves? The Rosenbergs lost themselves, in a very real sense. And even though a person may be able to stand off and look at the ridiculousness of his own petty strivings and his silly strutting, what will he do about it? Will insight lead to dedication? May it not as easily lead to depression? And concerning a philosophy of life, is it not too much of the mind? I would have much preferred to hear him say "a faith." A man may hold a philosophy of life—unconsciously, half-consciously, or fully consciously—and it may not make too much difference in his conduct or mental climate. But a faith holds him and makes him, or it twists him.

In time, perhaps, the religionist and the psychologist may

get together. They are together now up to a point, but beyond that there is divergence. The Christian at least, must always be saying, "What do ye more than others?"

THE BIBLE AND GROWTH

Compare these goals of the psychologist with the approach to the problems of growth as presented in the Bible. We are accustomed to thinking of books written a long time ago as being out-of-date and largely in error. So when we read the Word of God it is easy to fall into that habit of thinking. But the Bible authenticates itself generation after generation because of its fresh, realistic, and profound approach to human problems. It carries an ineradicable persuasion concerning its inspiration and its uniqueness, because it actually inspires and because it approaches the human situation as no other book or institution. It has stimulated stunted souls for almost 2000 years.

In the New Testament, for example, growth is the purpose of all of God's program for the Christian. Jesus said to his followers, "Be ye therefore perfect [mature], even as your Father which is in heaven is perfect." This is a remarkable concept. Man is to rise to the heights of God. At least, that is his stated goal. It is akin to the Old Testament doctrine of holiness: God, speaking to Moses and Aaron, instructed them to say to the people, "Ye shall therefore be holy, for I am holy." (Lev. 11:45). Norman Snaith, a modern Old Testament scholar, tells us that the word "holy" means what is without parallel. God is without parallel. So in the New Testament, the emphasis is on maturity, with Jesus as our one example of a fully grown person. As Shakespeare has Iago say to Othello, "He hath a daily beauty in his life that makes me ugly."

Put very plainly, holiness and maturity are not the dream of some starry-eyed preacher. They are magnificent concepts of the very nature of man. They rest upon the foundation of God's having created us in his image. We are made of the kind of stuff that is capable of responding to the upward call and of growing toward the unique Person.

Paul builds his whole system of doctrine around this growth ideal. In his letter to the Ephesians he writes of our lives as a "calling" or vocation. The concept is not an easy one to translate. It is more than insight and less than a voice from heaven. Paul seems to be denoting the true sense of mission which every Christian has increasingly as he grows. But his point is that all of Christ's redemptive program and all of the church's organization and methods aim at our maturity. Take this passage from the very heart of the epistle to the Ephesians for example:

And he has given us some men as apostles, some as prophets, some as missionaries, some as pastors and teachers, in order to fit his people for the work of service, for building the body of Christ, until we all attain unity in faith, and in the knowledge of the Son of God, and reach mature manhood, and that full measure of development found in Christ. We must not be babies any longer, blown about and swung around by every wind of doctrine through the trickery of men with their ingenuity in inventing error. We must lovingly hold to the truth and grow up into perfect union with him who is the head—Christ himself. For it is under his control that the whole system, adjusted and united by each ligament of its equipment, develops in proportion to the functioning of each particular part, and so builds itself up through love (Eph. 4: 11-16 Goodspeed).

This ideal of reaching "the full measure of development found in Christ" is a bold one. But he meant exactly that. In Romans 8: 29 he states the plan of God as a proposal to make all of us like his Son. We must not dilute this teaching and still call it Christianity. We are not only to follow Christ, to worship him, to sit at his feet, but we are to reach his degree of maturity.

The inspired apostle knew that growth was primarily an inner experience, so we find him saying such things as: "Brethren, do not be children in your thinking; be babes in evil, but in thinking be mature" (1 Cor. 14:20 RSV); "Let this mind be in you, which was also in Christ Jesus" (Phil. 2:25); "Him [Christ] we proclaim, warning every man and teaching every man in all wisdom, that we may present every man mature in Christ" (Col. 1:28 RSV).

So far as Paul's life was concerned, he summed up his own efforts in two passages. One is that remarkable poem on love in 1 Corinthians: "When I was a child, I spoke like a child, I thought like a child, I reasoned like a child; when I became a man, I gave up childish ways" (13:11 RSV). Perhaps he exaggerated a little, if we are to take him literally, for no person has given up all of his "childish ways." Paul clearly admits this in his letter to the Philippians: "Not that I have already obtained this [becoming like Christ] or am already perfect [full grown]. . . . But one thing I do, forgetting what lies behind and straining forward to what lies ahead, I press on toward the goal for the prize of the upward call of God in Christ Jesus" (3:12-14 RSV).

THE CHURCHES ARE INTERESTED

Perhaps these passages are sufficient to show that one great focus of the early churches was on growth and that it was personal and inward. If ever the churches needed this emphasis it is now. We are prone to measure the growth of Christianity by numbers, income, churches, or prestige of church members. We count Christians when we ought to measure them. How tall are they? Are they growing? Are they mature enough to follow Christ through the fires of persecution? Do they stand for something in an age when most people fall for almost anything, if it is cleverly presented?

It will become clearer in the discussions that follow what we mean by growth, how we grow, and the standards by which we may measure ourselves. At this point, it should be stated that the church is interested in the growth of the whole person. Nothing of importance can happen to a man without the discerning eye of the church. This does not mean that the church tries to force people into a mold or to build them by a blueprint. It does mean that the church tries to confront each person with the warm, strong personality of Christ saying, "Are you doing his will? Are you following his leadership in your daily life?"

The church has means for promoting growth. They are not unique, but they are central. We learned them from the Master himself. The first and the most important is example; it is the Christian's most effective teaching method. Then, there are the age-old means of teaching and proclaiming the good news of God's revelation to man. Even here the Christian approach stands alone; it depends upon insight, appreciation, and persuasion rather than upon fear, shame, and threats.

Most important among the Christian techniques is simple friendship and love. This love accepts people as they are, leaves them free to change, and furnishes the atmosphere of hope and joy. Love serves, solicits, sacrifices, all in order that human beings might come to experience the full life of growth for which they were intended.

In short, the church comes to the problem of human growth with some distinctive assets. It accepts all of the other contributions to growth without prejudice—at least, at its best it does. It has a definite ideal or goal toward which every individual may direct himself. At the same time Christian teachings foster the acceptance of individuals at any level or stage of development; and this acceptance neither settles down to complacency nor demands immediately the impossible. The church claims, also, to possess the means for growth as a part of its way of salvation: the creative Word, the divine guidance and power, the church fellowship, the regular worship services, and the challenge of a worldwide program.

Churches Assume Responsibility

Finally, the church is the only institution which interests itself in and assumes responsibility for growth at every period in life.

Children and the home are given a great deal of time and thought in the church's program. When homes are broken, or children are forced to work in sweat shops, or schools foster destructive programs, the church rises up and speaks its piece. When psychiatrists point out that mental illness can be prevented, the church examines its program and the items in our culture which may contribute to health and growth. In adolescence, in home building, in choosing a vocation, in the crises of middle age, in all of the problems of later maturity (formerly called "old age"), the church takes a sincere interest.

It does not propose to do all that needs to be done for man. The work of the schools, the medical and legal professions, the entertainment field, the government, are all not only accepted but encouraged. But every one of these will be judged by one criterion: Does it contribute to human growth? Monopolies, racial conflicts, wars, pornographic literature, drinking habits, competition, and every aspect of private and public life, in the church and in the market place, must be judged by whether it retards or accelerates human growth.

The church is necessarily committed to human growth because of its concept of human nature. Man is far from what he ought to be and is capable of unlimited growth. Every human resource must be used to create the atmosphere for growth; but then there are divine resources which may be used. If man were a mere animal, even though a glorified, thoughtful one, he could only become static and cease to grow. But if he is created to become, ultimately, like his Creator, he may continue to grow right down to the grave—and beyond. This is the faith of true Christian churches, and as long as they possess the truly creative power, they will be able to produce samples of their product. The vindication of faith in human growth is to be found, not in arguments nor in preachments, but in individuals who are growing.

If churches can produce Christians who experience a consistently healthy growth toward a worthy, desirable maturity goal, they have a real contribution to make to mankind. The wise individual will not ask what we were like when we started. It is enough to ask in what direction we are going and with what speed. For, however man may disguise it from himself, there is hardly anything for which every one of us hungers as much as for an enlarged and better self. To grow is one of our basic needs.

> We all are blind, until we see
>   That in the human plan
> Nothing is worth the making if
>   It does not make the man.
>
> Why build these cities glorious
>   If man unbuilded goes?
> In vain we build the work, unless
>   The builder also grows.[5]
>
> EDWIN MARKHAM

ARE YOU THE GROWING KIND? 2

WOODROW WILSON once said, "In Washington some men grow, while others just swell." It is not only in Washington but all over the world that there is a difference in men. An old carpenter once said to William James, "There is not much difference in men but what there is is important." One great difference lies in spiritual or personality growth. Some grow and others regress. None stand still or, at least, appear to. But most move back and forth in a sort of zigzag state of change which they assume, without thinking, to be progress.

If we look about us, we see growth, physical and social, most plainly evident in childhood and adolescence. We get our physical stature without thinking. Certain social adjustments are forced upon us if we move about in human society. We must learn to respect property rights, to wear clothes, to eat human food in a fairly human manner, to perform certain skills for livelihood, and to behave so as not to frighten our neighbors. We may even learn a minimum of social intercourse in order to secure a mate and to avoid ostracism in the community. But are these the goals of human life? Do these marginal requirements of life satisfy our deep needs?

Let us take a God's-eye view of ourselves and the whole world around us. All we see, whether we look up, around, or down, is persons and things. If this seems a little dogmatic— for we actually cannot see a person, only skin, hair, eyes, and other physical details—we may put all reality into the categories of the living and the nonliving.

LIFE A MYSTERY

This living classification comes close to human interest and desire. The scientist divides it into plant, animal, and human life. Or perhaps he prefers to remind us that all life has one watery, formless, and flowing substance. This chemical system, called protoplasm, mysterious as it is, is necessary to all physical life, from the one living cell to the highly complex man. Dr. Edmund W. Sinnott, director of the Sheffield Scientific School and dean of the Graduate School at Yale University, in a most remarkable book called *Cell and Psyche,* says: [1]

For all men life must nevertheless remain the ultimate problem. Around it, since we ourselves are living things, center those great questions which have stirred mankind most deeply. . . . The structure of the atom, the size of space, and the theory of relativity interest a few, but rarely stir men deeply. . . . But those more vital matters, which reach into our hearts as much as into our minds, have set wars ablaze and banners flying and poets singing and mystics praying since the dawn of history. These are all problems of *life,* and life is the ultimate mystery.

If some legalistic mind were to insist on a definition of life, we could only make the answer that A. E. Housman made when asked to define poetry: "Neither can a cat define a rat, but he knows one when he sees it." Actually, it is not that simple. Some philosophers think of the universe as alive.

From a human standpoint to be alive means self-consciousness; we must be aware of ourselves. But does it? We are alive when we are asleep or delirious.

Life is a mystery, too complex to be encased in our little cartons of words. We can merely point to it and say, "Life does thus and so—usually."

How Life Behaves

Life organizes. The biologists have a very happy word which emphasizes this great fact, "organism." When man is spoken of as being made up of certain chemicals, that is of significance only if you intend to use him as fertilizer. The really important fact is that a microscopic cell of one two-hundred-and-fiftieth of an inch in size can develop into a whale, a man, or a mouse, depending on something guiding it from within. A minute protoplasmic disc, on the yolk of a bird's egg develops, for example, into a respectable chick within twenty-one days. It then contains billions of cells grouped into many different organs ranging from a deeply sensitive brain and nerves to inert feathers. Whatever (or whoever) directs this process, its primary characteristic is that it moves constantly toward a particular kind of goal or system. (See how inadequate our words are?)

Life grows. Dead things may accumulate, but they do not grow.

Sometimes this growth involves enlargement, as a sprout into a tree, or a baby into an adult. But not always. It may involve simple and constant renewal. The breaking-down and building-up processes, known together by the name of metabolism, is going on all of the time in a living body. In youth the building-up process, or anabolism, is in the lead. As the organism ages, the breaking-down process, catabolism, dominates; and then, at a given point, death occurs. This is the story of one aspect of physical growth.

Growth sometimes takes place in a disorderly and purposeless way. I refer to cancerous growth. Here we have an unexplained operation by which some cells flare up into a spurt of wild growth, overrunning, choking, and finally killing the rest of the body. Living cells are orderly, co-operative cells. Cancer cells merely increase in number without helping to form lungs, heart, or brain.

Life involves reproduction. In its simpler forms one cell divides and two individual cells are formed. In more highly developed organisms, what the biologists call "regeneration" takes place. You can cut off a tadpole's tail or leg and a new one, similar in every way to the one removed, will grow out. You can cut an angleworm in two and the head end will grow a new tail. Healing of wounds and recovery from starvation involve this same process of regeneration.

Life in every form must come from life. One living being must give rise to another of its kind. No living thing has ever been known to arise directly from nonliving matter. There are many varied methods of reproduction in nature but reproduction there must be, where there is life.

Finally, life must be sustained from without. Living things eat. They are transformers of energy and matter. No life is self-perpetuating. It is true that there are substances which speed up growth and control the use of food, but food of an appropriate kind is necessary to life. All life is dependent.

In the human species, for example, there is a gland at the base of the brain called the pituitary gland, which determines the growth of the human body. If this gland does not produce enough of a certain hormone, the child never grows up but remains a dwarf. If it is overactive, we have a body of enormous frame. The doctors call this gigantism.

THE MEANING OF HUMAN GROWTH

There are many things about the way life and growth take place that even the best scientist does not propose to understand. But we need to remember that the life process, through which a human being goes naturally, is made up of organized growth, enlargement, renewal, reproduction, aging, and death. The very fact that this process is a mystery which we experience as change, development, freedom, and yet order— not a static, mechanical process—makes us value the word "life" and apply it to our spiritual experiences.

Growth is sometimes used to mean simply adding one to one, as in the growth of a man's capital. But when we are thinking of the human personality, growth is a figure of speech, and we need to remember that. We use it to mean that self within a man which may be ever enlarging, renewing, reproducing, organizing—we might even say aging and dying.

It is at this point that we need to suspect the growth figure. Do people necessarily get senile spiritually? They change, but need they grow old? Or, for that matter, does the Bible teach that the spirit of man, by nature (that is, without the intervention of God), may be capable of growth?

Of course, in every type of physical life, there is a maximal growth limit. Even men afflicted with gigantism never grow to be twenty feet tall. And there seems to be a relationship between the length of the maturity period and the length of life. In most animals it is about five times the length of the maturity period. A human being, for example, takes about twenty years to mature and hardly lives beyond the hundred-year mark. As one author puts it:

The newly born guinea pig can shift for himself three days after birth. Man is set apart from other animals by the protracted period of infancy and childhood. Nearly one third of man's life span is spent in preparation for living the latter two thirds.... He is essentially a learning animal, and biologically speaking he develops so slowly that his mental processes are enabled to use and absorb the cumulative experiences of all that have gone before him.

From the time of conception to death, physical growth, as we have defined it to include metabolism, takes place. But physical life has its limits.

THE BIBLE AND THE LIFE OF THE SOUL

It would be easy to use physical growth as an analogy and to assume that all a man needs to do spiritually is to keep outreaching and renewing until death overtakes him. Man is a child of God and simply needs to lift his head toward the sun, we hear people say. But is this Jesus' conception? Is this in accord with the New Testament?

Quite the contrary seems to be true. It is death rather than life which reigns in this world, the Bible says. Some people go through life producing bad fruit. Or some never produce fruit for God, as it is stated in other passages. Before we can grow spiritually, we must be alive spiritually. Life is used in a distinctive sense, not wholly unlike its usual sense, when the New Testament speaks of it. And growth, then, is the unfolding and expressing of this new life which God mysteriously gives to us. This puts growth on a higher level.

At this point, we shall not attempt to describe how spiritual growth takes place but to show that the divine life is necessary to growth.

Jesus is presented in the New Testament as the true life, the giver of life, the sustainer of life, and the only victor over death. "In him was life; and the life was the light of men" (John 1:4). "For as the Father hath life in himself; so hath he given to the Son to have life in himself" (John 5:26). "For the bread of God is he which cometh down from heaven, and giveth life unto the world" (John 6:33). "I am come that they might have life, and that they might have it more abundantly" (John 10:10). "But these are written, that ye might believe that Jesus is the Christ, the Son of God; and that believing ye might have life through his name" (John 20:31).

Matthew and Luke recorded the Master's words when he used another figure. "Do men gather grapes of thorns, or figs of thistles? Even so every good tree bringeth forth good fruit; but a corrupt tree bringeth forth evil fruit. A good tree cannot bring forth evil fruit, neither can a corrupt tree bring forth good fruit. Every tree that bringeth not forth good fruit is hewn down, and cast into the fire" (Matt. 7:16-19). It is not alleged that there is not a kind of life in all men, but it is affirmed that good living comes from a certain kind of good life. "Each after its kind" is a law of nature and of God. Sometimes it is called merely life; again, and often in John, it is called eternal life.

"Ye must be born again" were the words Jesus used in confronting Nicodemus with the new life. On another occasion he likened the living experience to a branch attached to the main stem of the vine: "I am the vine, ye are the branches: He that abideth in me, and I in him, the same bringeth forth much fruit: for without me ye can do nothing" (John 15:5). The most frequent figure used by Paul was that of the resurrection. We are dead in sins until we are made alive by our experience in Christ (Eph. 2:1-10). "In Christ shall all be made alive" (1 Cor. 15:22).

Other New Testament writers and passages might be cited, but the teaching is plain: Life is available to all who will receive it and this life comes from God through Christ. It is full —abundant; it is eternal—the life of God; and it is the only basis for growth.

In every living being there seems to be some inner regulator or director, a kind of self-regulator. Else how does a plant or an animal develop into its full self? Neither the scientist nor the philosopher seems to know what to call it. Perhaps there are forces or regulators in man which have been marred or destroyed by sin so that he cannot become what he was intended without a regeneration or an overhauling.

What else could the new birth mean, except that God somehow changes man so that he has a new director, to use the scientist's word? It means that a great leap forward may be made by the divine act. "If any one is in Christ, he is a new creation" (2 Cor. 5: 17 RSV). He has new potentialities which will develop normally, as all life does, if only man will yield to the conditions for growth.

Religion, then, means for the Christian not simply becoming the best that the natural man can become; but it means receiving a new life, the life of God. That is the beginning. Nothing divine can be expected to grow unless there is the divine life to start with.

THE MAN IN THE BASEMENT 3

DID you ever go down into an old fashioned basement of a house and look at the accumulation of the years? I am not thinking of the modern basements with recreation rooms and bars. The old basements in large homes were the storerooms for such things as baby high chairs, trunks, empty fruit jars, broken rocking chairs, old bedsteads, family heirlooms, discarded family portraits, camping equipment, dog harnesses, and parts of many things from many places.

If you walk around with a flashlight in your hand in such a basement, your mind is crowded with a hundred associated memories. Some of the objects might bring tears, some laughter, some a wry smile. As the spotlight falls on each object, you remember things and events which have long been shelved in your mind. Some of them, perhaps, you would like to forget. Some bring back very tender and cherished memories. We are a part of all we have met.

I am thinking that in every person there is something that corresponds roughly to a basement. It is a part of us, just as the basement is a part of the house. We may not be aware of what is in this part of ourselves, but it is there just the same. It is related to ourselves and our past. The real difference is

22

that this part of us is not like old broken rockers and fishing tackle—still and unobtrusive; this part of us is dynamic, alive, and constantly giving us trouble. The man in the basement knocks on the door to get out, steals through the basement windows, and demands constant watching.

FREUD AND PAUL

The importance of our secret self was first brought forcefully to my attention years ago when I read, from the pen of Halford Luccock of Yale Divinity School, the statement that the modern psychologist, Sigmund Freud, was probably "closer to Paul than any other modern writer, including all the theologians." Both emphasized the constant and necessary war within the personality. Both saw the deep, disturbing depravity of man. Both saw that life consists of adjustments which the individual makes in the midst of conflict.

Freud was not a Christian, but as a scientist he arrived at this sort of a view of man. We come into the world equipped with certain instincts or drives or motivating forces. The little baby does not know the difference between himself and "the other than himself." He has all sorts of drives: tenderness, hunger, anger, curiosity, and so on. The child is extremely selfish and demanding. As he grows from infancy he finds that these crude desires must be conditioned. He must become civilized.

The civilizing force within the personality is the conscience or super-ego. It is a kind of judge or super-parent who says, "Thou shalt not" or "Thou shalt." It is more, actually. In the process of life development the conscience not only forbids a deed but even denies that such a desire is present. At least, some force within the personality holds down the impulses both by conscious effort and by unconscious denial.

Many people think that religion is allied with the conscience, so they spend their lives trying to obey rules and to make other people obey them. The revelation of God, to them, is the revelation of his will—as in the Ten Commandments for example. Such people have little mercy or goodness. They spend their lives trying to be good, and nobody believes in their goodness except themselves.

Between the conscience and the instincts or impulses, for Freud and most modern psychologists, is the conscious self. The ego, it is called. It consists of will-power, reason, and love, the really human and good part of man. The conscious self serves as a kind of arbiter between the lower self and the higher self or conscience. What we are, they say, depends on ego strength, upon the self-directing, thinking, deciding part of the human personality.

Now a great part of this whole process of the individual's behavior is unconscious. Most of the instinctual life is. A part of the conscience is. The mind is like an iceberg, nine-tenths of it is under water and one-tenth visible to the human eye. Thus, there is much of mystery in all of us.

I remember that at the Yale School of Alcohol Studies a member of the class said to a well-known psychiatrist: "Dr. Tiebout, if the human personality is somewhat as you describe, isn't an understanding of the unconscious and an acceptance and conscious control of our impulses all we need?" Dr. Tiebout's reply was, "God pity the man who thinks he understands his unconscious." He went on to show how the alcoholic, like anyone else, needs a Power greater than himself to manage his complex personality.

You see, religion aims at the conscious self. It is not on the side of the conscience as is commonly supposed. It is on the side of the ego. It aims at building a balanced person, at strengthening controls which do not leave him weak or in the thick of battle constantly, but help him make an adjustment which enables him to give his life in service to God and man.

The key words of the Christian faith are peace, joy, freedom, love, truth, and faith. But the first three can never be achieved as long as either the instinct or the conscience is in control. It is only as love for other people, the truth of God as revealed in Christ, and a faith-surrender to him become dominant in our lives that we are free and, at the same time, controlled.

MENTAL ILLNESS

By way of parenthesis, I should like to point out also that mental illness, which is such a great problem in our day, is not a sign of badness or lack of faith. Illness occurs when the normal, automatic ego controls are not working well. The conflict between the impulses and the conscience is not being handled properly. It may be that the conscience is too severe (for it is not trustworthy), or the childish desires too strong, or the conscious organization of the personality faulty through ignorance or lack of love. In any case, to judge a person who is emotionally ill is contrary to both science and religion.

For example, a young doctor told one of my students that he had never seen a real Christian on a psychiatric ward. That is the height of prejudice and stupidity! Some of the best people I have ever known have had emotional disorders. And I have seen some great Christians who were temporarily insane. People become mentally ill when their repressions get out of hand or their method of personality organization is not successful. To blame the person for that is unkind, unwarranted, and unchristian.

What, then, is the approach of religion to handling this problem of living with ourselves? It is two-fold. The Christian faith tries to acquaint man with his true nature and to persuade him to allow God to help him manage it. As stated before, put in modern terms, religion aims at the conscious self. This self must deal with many problems which grow out of the instinctual drives, or the unconscious; but also with an equal number which grow out of the scoldings or pamperings of a distorted conscience. It is the conscious self which is responsible to God and can be judged by God only; which can be born again and grow into Christlikeness. How God performs these miracles, no one can fully explain. But the whole problem of salvation and Christianity is bringing this man in the basement under control and into co-operation with God.

JESUS ON HUMAN NATURE

Read the words of Jesus on this subject: "And he said, 'What comes out of a man is what defiles a man. For from within, out of the heart of man, come evil thoughts, fornication, theft, murder, adultery, coveting, wickedness, deceit, licentiousness, envy, slander, pride, foolishness. All these evil things come from within, and they defile a man'" (Mark 7: 20-23 RSV).

This passage grew out of a defense Jesus was offering for his disciples. They were not observing all of the Jewish ceremonial cleansing rituals, such as washing the hands to the elbows before eating—this was before the day of information about microbes, so was purely a religious ritual. The Master's attitude was extremely radical, in the light of his times. But the important part of the defense, for us, is his list of the evils which spring from within the human heart. He was saying that moral failures are more important than ceremonial failures. They are what really harm the human personality, "defile man"; and the human spirit is God's chief concern.

Look at the names he gives to these destructive traits. Evil thoughts mean the planning of evil without regard to God's will, as in David's dealing with Bathsheba. Fornication and adultery apply to sexual immorality, and licentiousness to "over-sexuality." "Murder" and "theft" are obvious. Coveting is the itch to have more, the "have more" attitude, and grows out of a response to a corrupt culture. Wickedness is just plain meanness and probably designates what moderns would call "criminality." Deceit is another kind of criminality—dishonesty in business—or may even apply to social deception. An evil eye is the sin of jealousy in a highly competitive society. Slander is the product of a vicious tongue used in some way to hurt someone else. Pride is holding oneself above others and above what God intended. And, finally, foolishness is an anti-climax word which probably includes most of the others; it means no moral sense.

This list of sins is quite inclusive. All of them are antisocial ones and bring suffering and sorrow in their wake. Jesus' concept of what defiles man is a far cry from the useless religious rules and compulsive rituals of the Jews of his day. Not one of these sins has to do with ceremony or religious dogma. And the point which we must not overlook is that these debasing patterns of living come from within. They spring from human nature; they are rooted in the very egoistic structure of our infantile selves.

A little five-year-old boy, the child of a friend, surprised his parents and his neighbors by hitting a neighbor boy in the head with a rock. He was frightened and ashamed. His explanation was: "Daddy, I don't know how to explain it, but this is the way it happened. A voice seemed to say to me, 'Go ahead and throw it'; and another voice, 'Don't do it,' and somehow I went ahead and threw it." His father was rather firm in his objection to the voice theory, but it is a very old one. However, the Bible puts it this way: "Every man is tempted, when he is drawn away of his own lust, and enticed" (James 1: 14).

This is no attempt to say that man is all bad. Rather, it states frankly that evil does not spring simply from one's culture or from bad social patterns, but from the very center of each individual life.

PAUL'S VIEW OF THE FLESH

A similar concept is presented by the apostle Paul in his letter to the Galatians. Here he contrasts the struggle of the spirit against the "flesh." It is fairly evident from reading this letter, or the one to the Romans, that by "Spirit" the writer does not mean simply "our higher selves" but the Holy Spirit. This is clear when we remember that the Spirit of God dwells in every true Christian; he has been born of the Spirit and made a member of the body of Christ.

So Paul says that the flesh is the mainspring of evil. Marshall points out that by flesh Paul means "what we mean today when we speak of the natural impulses and instincts which, while they are not sinful in themselves, master us and become occasions of sin unless we master them." Or more accurately, they master us when we are cut off from the redeeming power of God.

But how does the flesh express itself? Paul says that "the works of the flesh are plain: immorality, impurity, licentiousness, idolatry, sorcery, enmity, strife, jealousy, anger, selfishness, dissension, party spirit, envy, drunkenness, carousing, and the like. I warn you, as I warned you before, that those who do such things shall not inherit the kingdom of God" (Gal. 5: 19-21 RSV).

A close look at this list of fourteen bad behavior patterns

shows that they may easily fall into four classes: (1) sex; (2) false religion; (3) hostility; and (4) intemperance. The first three obviously apply to irresponsibility in sex life. The next two concern all sorts of heathen practices which put images and magic as a prominent part of religion. The third group includes the largest list of sins (eight), and all are a violation of the spirit of love; they have to do with what we speak of today as interpersonal or human relations. The fourth, which includes the last two items on the list, are both words which apply to group drinking. In their social structure there probably was no "solo" drinking, as we have in our Western culture. In any case, the drinking led to intoxication which needs no argument to prove its degrading effect.

As Dr. A. T. Robertson says, this is "a lively list" of sins. Lively and earthy, and it is interesting to note that the Roman Catholic official list of "seven deadly sins" includes two, "gluttony" and "laziness," which are not included in either of these. I prefer Jesus' and Paul's.

But to call these "lists of sins" is almost to miss the point. They are more nearly attempts to tell the nature of man by suggesting how he acts. You tell what is in a well by the kind of liquid the pump produces. Some of us would like to divorce ourselves from our natures, jump out of our skins, and blame our sins on Satan, on our parents who represent our early training, or on our culture. This seems like very superficial psychology and anthropology to me. As Emil Brunner points out, "Christian anthropology regards man as not only responsible but also as guilty." He is "neither animal nor divine."

It would be easy for some of us to agree with Jesus' and Paul's description of human nature and say that "there are a lot of people in the world like that." Like the woman who said to the preacher, "Wonderful sermon! Everything you said applies to somebody or other I know."

Look Around and Within

As we look closely, however, at ourselves, our neighbors, and even at our families, we find some of these same characteristics present. Is any one of us free from covetousness or envy or pride or selfishness? H. G. Wells, in *The Holy Terror,* writes: "Man has become a new animal who can jump a hundred miles, see through a brick wall, bombard the atom, and analyse the stars, yet he goes on behaving like the weak, quarrelsome ape he used to be." Bishop Creighton has said, "Whenever you have got the ape and the tiger out of people there still remains the donkey, a much more stubborn animal." We speak of our "animal natures," but we must not forget that they are a part of ourselves. It may be that they are the part of us to which Shakespeare referred in the thirty-first sonnet, "things removed, that hidden in thee lie."

Perhaps we can see this part of ourselves more clearly if we translate what Paul called "the flesh" into modern terms. The man in the basement is dealt with in modern psychology as well as in the Bible. But even the language of the child may describe him. Such a prominent part of reality does not need technical language to contain it.

Characteristics of the Secret Self

The man in the basement is *a selfish child*. Dr. Leon Saul says that "within every grown-up lives the little child he once was." This is no reflection on children. It is natural for them to make demands, to attempt to dominate, to seek pleasure only, to be jealous, to act out their impulses. But this self-centered, I-want-my-way, why-doesn't-someone-love-me attitude is within everyone of us from the bassinet to the mortuary.

This secret self is, also, *a killer*. Some of the most saintly people I have ever known, when they were hurt deeply, hated violently. They may cover it up with politeness or camouflage it with coldness, but it is hate just the same. "The urge to kill" is deep within every human being. A little child will say, "I hate you; I could kill you." An older person reacts to the same murderous impulse by fearing another will die. It is a fact that borne out by many clinical studies that great anxiety concerning another's death is often caused by an unconscious wish that he might die. Likewise, suicide is often shown to be the result of hostility toward someone else that gets turned inward toward the self.

This baby, basement self seeks, under all circumstances, to *avoid pain*. "Don't hurt me" is its slogan. Therefore, when this self is in control, the individual never has the courage to stand for something. He had rather be "an innocent bystander." Religion to him is an escape, and he will not accept any other. No crosses for him, unless someone else dies on it, like Christ. The path of least resistance is the royal road to heaven for him. If he suffers, he takes a drink to relax him. He "passes the buck," but he never bucks the line. "O please go way and let me sleep" is his theme song.

Quite an unexpected, and very subtle, bit of unconscious behavior—at least, springing from the unconscious—is *humor*. The man in the basement laughs at the man upstairs (the conscience). Humor is the mercy the conscience shows to the fleshly self. We laugh at those who kick over the traces. Which side are we on? The side of morality or of sin? Everyone knows that sexy jokes "lay them in the aisles"—some audiences, at least; even some very nice people. For the moment of laughter we are identified with the "superior" viewpoint which is unmoral, and we show mercy to our instincts. That is why humor is one of the most revealing facts about an individual. Only really good people can afford to laugh. For the remainder, it dulls the edge of moral discrimination. Good humor, then, is a blessing, in that we all need some mercy. But bad humor is either vulgar, cruel, vindictive, or downright silly.

Finally, the man in the basement is *burning up with ambition*. He intends to get ahead, God or no God. His associates are competitors instead of collaborators. His way of life is rivalism instead of mutualism. James and John, coming to Jesus, asking to sit "one on thy right hand, and the other on the left" in his kingdom, are a perfect illustration. Their egocentric selves were in charge during this interview. The will to power even enters into religion and is sometimes very difficult to discern.

Now what has this picture of man's inner, lower, impulsive self to do with growth? Does it matter what we think about the flesh or the heart? Our interest is not in an analysis of the nature or essence of man, as much as it is in understanding how he behaves. In modern jargon, we are concerned about "what makes him tick." This leads inevitably to a concept of what man is in himself. And can anyone observe his neighbors and question the realism of the New Testament?

How Growth Takes Place

Growth, then, is concerned with progress in dealing with these objectionable impulses. This world is a very hard place for a "baby" who never becomes an adult. When people "act out" their impulses or hold on to childish patterns of living, they are headed for sorrow and distress. The viewpoint of the New Testament, it seems, is that salvation does not deliver a person from the fleshly self. Nor does it propose simply to strengthen his conscience so that he may "hold down," by fear and inhibitions, the wild desires—keep the basement door shut, so to speak. This cannot be done. Growth consists in the strengthening of our conscious controls.

Christ allies himself with the ego or conscious self. His is not a religion of rules and punishment, like Judaism and Mohammedanism, as well as popular paganism. Nor is it an escapism into mystic trances or separation from the world. To go further, Christ does not propose to transform or redeem the unconscious, as E. Stanley Jones and some others claim. All one has to do to know that a Christian's unconscious is not redeemed is to examine his dreams, or watch him become insane, or even catch him off guard when he is frustrated. The unconscious takes over in these cases. Christ saves the whole person, of course, but the unconscious or impulsive life is not destroyed. It is held down, controlled by the Spirit of God working through the Christian. We must learn to live with the man in the basement and keep him under control. Growth is the increasingly smooth control of that aggressive, untamed part of self.

THE CHRISTIAN VIEW

What is the Christian solution to handling the instinctual self? I believe that there is a divine way and there is a human way. The human way includes indulgence, will-power, self-destruction (as in Buddhism), and auto-suggestion (the "positive thinking" relaxation cults). But the Christian way is one of dependence upon God, from start to finish. No mental tricks, no mysterious rituals. It seems to be contained in three experiences which I shall merely mention.

The first one is "death." "And those who belong to Christ Jesus have crucified the flesh with its passions and desires"

(Gal. 5:24 RSV). "Put to death therefore what is earthly in
you: immorality, impurity, passion, evil desire, and covetousness, which is idolatry" (Col. 3:5 RSV). Other passages might
be quoted but these state clearly the Christian view.

Well, one says, if we are to "crucify the flesh," let us get busy
and destroy the man in the basement. Yes, let us! But like
the proverbial cat, he has a number of lives. We can never quite
destroy him. These death figures are symbols of the experience
the Christian has of bringing himself to Christ, unconscious
and all, and saying, "Here I am; I renounce all loyalties except
to you; you may have the keys to all of the rooms of my house;
cause me to die to sin but to live unto righteousness." Or something like that. At any rate, a cross is involved. We accept this
death concept just as we do the words of our Master, "Be ye
therefore perfect, even as your Father which is in heaven is
perfect." In fact, they are two sides of the same experience.

The second aspect of dealing with our drives is to accept the
conflict. Those who do not wish to live in conflict are not made
for this world. Paul describes his own "struggle of the soul"
in Romans 7:

> I do not understand my own actions. For I do not do what I want, but
> I do the very thing I hate. Now if I do what I do not want, I agree that
> the law is good. So then it is no longer I that do it, but sin which dwells
> within me. For I know that nothing good dwells within me, that is, in
> my flesh. I can will what is right, but I cannot do it. For I do not do
> the good I want, but the evil I do not want is what I do. Now if I do
> what I do not want, it is no longer I that do it, but sin which dwells
> within me (Rom. 7:15-20 RSV).

He concludes the passage by thanking God for the victory
through Jesus Christ. The Christian wins, but he never de-
stroys the foe.

There are stories of ancient tyrants who forced those guilty
of murder to suffer an offensive punishment. The dead body

was chained to the murderer in such a way that he was forced to bear it until it had completely rotted away. This may have been what Paul had in mind when he said, "Wretched man that I am! Who will deliver me from this body of death?" (Rom. 7:24 RSV).

It is at the point of struggling with the flesh that religion and psychiatry meet. Both are interested in strengthening the ego or conscious self. Psychiatry deals with people whose conscious controls are more seriously impaired; they are emotionally sick.

Let us illustrate it this way. A certain clinical psychologist states that the unconscious forces may be likened to a large number of rats in a basement. All openings are closed except one from the basement to the kitchen. If we allow them to come out one at a time, we may be able to kill them. But if a number rush through the opening at once we are overwhelmed, confused, and disturbed. If for some reason he has to face too many decisions, too much unconscious material comes through, his anxiety greatly increases, he must seek ways of defending himself, and thereby becomes sick.

Religion does not propose to cure insanity any more than it does cancer or tuberculosis, but it aids. Actually, the right kind of religion, one that is realistic, intelligent, and loving, may do a great deal to strengthen the ego. It has been doing it for centuries. That is why it has been called "the psychiatry of the masses." But, unless the conscious controls are broken, man is responsible to God for "living in conflict" and making such decisions as he is capable of making. Only people who have a great deal of "struggle" are good Christians in God's sight. In other words, since our "enemies" are constant, we must either stay on the firing line or sink into complacency and spiritual inertia. Those who are fighting in the Christian manner are growing.

THE SPIRIT AND THE FLESH

The final insight into successful control of the flesh is to live by the Spirit. "Practice living by the Spirit and then by no means will you gratify the cravings of the lower nature" (Gal. 5: 16 Williams). Herbert Spencer has well said, "You cannot get golden conduct out of leaden instincts." Most of us do about as well as we may be expected to do without God's help. But the point here is that we need not be without his help. When we become Christians by the creative act of God's Spirit, we have just begun. The secret of growth in spiritual living is to be found in conscious dependence on the Holy Spirit, just as we depend on a strong parental hand to lead us when we are young.

The theologian has little advantage over the novice in understanding how God leads us. Both must learn by experience, and this comes about by a humble soul opening itself to God as a flower opens to the sunshine and fresh air. In ways that cannot be analyzed or explained, God gives strength, aids judgment, suggests new pathways. Our task is to learn to follow his leading, as the leaf follows the breeze.

I do not believe that anyone, psychologist or any other, can tell exactly how "living by the Spirit" strengthens the character and personality. It is evident, however, to anyone who has closely observed the development of sincere Christians that real stamina comes to those who follow this technique. There are times when such Christians are not sure which promptings come from the Holy Spirit and which from their own unconscious. But their very seeking and asking for God's help is itself both a growth stimulus and the result of growth. It clips the wings of pride and builds a bulwark against the onslaught of temptation. "For as many as are led by the Spirit of God, they are the sons of God" (Rom. 8: 14).

THE MAN UPSTAIRS 4

THERE is a scene in Paul Wellman's novel, *The Chain,* in which two of his characters are in a very intimate conversation about some of the great issues of life.[1]

"There *is* an unseen world," he told her. "Everyone's familiar with one common manifestation of it. Take a thought, an idea, whatever you want to call it. You can neither see, feel, nor test it by any sense. Still, it's there. Inescapably so. Thoughts are entities, and you create by the very act of thinking. Ideas you create have their proof in the fact that they create results. An idea is an entity, and an entity is a reality. If you and I, sitting here, can create a reality, it argues at least for the hypothesis of a Creator of the universe, and it argues also for other things beyond the reach of our physical and mental limitations."

He paused and picked up his cup again. She had been watching the brilliant play of his eyes, the way his features lit up as he spoke to her. He saw it, and said apologetically:

"This must be rather tiresome to you. Forgive me."

"It's nothing of the kind! I'm immensely interested by you."

He drank his cup, and said:

"Thank you. That preamble brings me back to the question of the conscience we were discussing and my conviction that it is something real and present—an actual organ of spiritual progress, as the brain is the organ of thought. Conscience, to my mind, is the perceptive power given us by God, at once admonitory and judicial guide to our actions. It tells us by instinct what's right and wrong, and, if it is followed, insures every man and woman growth in perfection of the spirit."

37

She considered this with a kind of zest, smiling within herself, but not derisively.

Similar conversations have taken place between millions of people for at least thirty centuries. Conscience has been connected with God. Lord Byron said, "Man's conscience is the oracle of God." This is an almost universal delusion and has done more harm to the children of men than can possibly be estimated.

What Is Conscience?

Closely akin to the above error is that one about conscience telling us, as Wellman's character put it, "by instinct what's right and wrong." I wish this were true. Life would be much simpler. But the truth is, finding out what is "right and wrong" is one of man's most perplexing problems—whether he listens to an inner voice or goes to an altar.

On one thing we may all agree. Conscience is "an actual organ of spiritual progress," a means for "growth in perfection of the spirit." In other words, conscience is man's most distinctive quality and his greatest inner problem. The way he deals with conscience will probably, more than any other single factor, determine whether he grows or declines spiritually. If his conscience is deformed, he cannot help but be a damaged soul. If it is good, he will at least be useful and, perhaps, happy and serene. The question of what is a good conscience is one of the most significant questions to be asked by any human being. Huck Finn defined it as that part of a person that "takes up more room than all the rest of a person's insides."

Which part? It is almost absurd to talk about where the conscience is located. But man cannot talk without using figures of speech. We speak of "the higher self," "the subconscious," "the super-ego." And a man jokes about "the little fellow who

is always sitting on my shoulder and whispering in my ear."
We fight with conscience, knock it down, and even kill it.

In order to be perfectly aware of the fact that we are using
a figure of speech, let us call conscience "the man upstairs."
He certainly stands in opposition to the instinctual life which
we have called "the man in the basement." All we could possibly mean, to be very honest, is that functioning of the human
person which values, condemns, approves, and even compels
the self.

We may be thoroughly figurative and say that the instinctual self acts like a criminal which lives in the basement
but is always clamoring for admission to the main floor, to the
living room. The conscience is the judge who lives upstairs,
watches out the second-floor window, warns against evil,
passes sentence when laws are not obeyed, and claims to be
infallible in his judgments. The conscious self rattles around
on the main floor, works, plays, makes decisions, dreams, lusts,
and accepts punishment or reward.

Is this human personality? Hardly. Man is much more uni-
fied than such a picture would indicate, and more complex.

There is in all normal human beings, however, a kind of
"automatic justice-maker." At least, it seems to be automatic
in adults and near adults. Alan Richardson says, "Every human being who is not clearly imbecile has a knowledge of
right and wrong." He "feels the obligation to do right, even
though he may perhaps hardly ever do it." Call it the moral
law within, the voice of God, an innate sense of morals, or
what you will. It is known especially for its condemning
qualities. King Richard cries:

> My conscience hath a thousand several tongues,
> And every tongue brings in a several tale,
> And every tale condemns me for a villain.
>   *King Richard III,* Act V, scene 3

CAN IT BE TRUSTED?

Is this man upstairs not as just and helpful as has been supposed? Is he to be suspected? Can he be explained away as the product of "what you were told before you were five years of age"? If the "judge" says that it is all right to ignore a particular call or to indulge in a favorite pleasure, are we to start quibbling? If a person feels that his "censor" approves, can he be very far wrong?

These are some of the questions which puzzle the mind and cause it to become "armoured and concluded." It would be hard to find a subject upon which more human beings refuse to be intelligent than that of conscience. To trust our feelings about right and wrong is an economy move. It takes effort to always be thinking and deciding. Besides, how would demagogues keep the masses under control if they did not appeal to the man upstairs for help?

I said to a woman of another faith not long ago, "You can investigate for yourself and see that what your religious leaders have told you will not stand up historically." She replied very sincerely, "I don't have to investigate; my conscience tells me that I am on the right track. You see, we believe that the conscience can be trusted, and I have been given the gift of faith to believe that." What can you do with a person who has so insulated herself against the God-given means of knowledge?

The woman's conscience had told her not to admit any possibility of change. That is what conscience often does, it blocks growth. It creates fear and forces the person to develop abnormal defenses against it. It does that as often as it pushes one out into new and more wholesome ways of life. Religious fanaticism is bred of a bad conscience. The fanatic must fight others because he has no peace within, and the fighting makes him more sure of himself.

Conscience Keeps Us from God

Emil Brunner, the noted European theologian, has put this very clearly: [2]

Conscience does not speak of God, but it is the flaming sword which drives us away from the presence of God. . . . Conscience is the fear of God—in the sense of the "fear that hath torment"—hence it drives the soul away from God, and yet it is also the longing of the soul for God; but it so distorts the way back to God that the soul can see nothing clearly; the soul does not know that it is God of whom it is afraid and for whom it longs.

Anyone who has done much religious counseling knows what Brunner means by "the flaming sword which drives us away from the presence of God." People often feel too guilty to pray. They say, "God seems to be a million miles away." Or a person feels uncomfortable at church, not because of what the preacher actually says, but because his conscience "just gives him fits" unless he is wholly surrendered—and that means to him an impossible way of life. Or a fine Christian man will not take a job, such as teaching a class of boys, because he is over-identified with perfection. The man upstairs demands perfection as a qualification of acceptance, thus preventing the person from serving in spite of his limitations.

These examples could be multiplied. There is hardly a religious problem which man faces that is not directly connected with a distorted conscience. And the sad part is that so few people dare think about how the conscience operates and how it may be educated. They feel like a little boy tampering with the mainspring of his father's watch. Many such people have consciences which require that they be realistic about everything except the conscience itself. If such people had nothing but the New Testament itself, they should know that conscience cannot be trusted.

THE PHARISAIC CONSCIENCE

The Pharisees are a classic example. They attached great importance to trivial matters. The keeping of little rules about walking a limited distance on the sabbath, ceremonially washing the hands before meals, tithing even the seasoning which went into foods, fasting (especially when it gave the secondary reward of publicity), and almsgiving, were for them matters of real conscientiousness. But caring for one's aged parents, showing mercy to impulse-ridden individuals, comforting the fallen, respecting the heretic, and even tolerating those who disagreed with them were matters which they tossed over into the pragmatic field. See how Jesus upbraided them:

Now the Pharisees gathered to meet him, with some scribes who had come from Jerusalem. They noticed that some of his disciples ate their food with 'common' (that is, unwashed) hands. (The Pharisees and all the Jews decline to eat, till they wash their hands up to the elbow, in obedience to the tradition of the elders; they decline to eat what comes from the market, till they have washed it; and they have a number of other traditions to keep about washing cups and jugs and basins and beds.) Then the Pharisees and scribes put this question to him, "Why do your disciples not follow the tradition of the elders? Why do they take their food with 'common' hands?" He said to them, "Yes, it was about you hypocrites indeed that Isaiah prophesied!—as it is written, *This people honours me with their lips, but their heart is far away from me: vain is their worship of me, for the doctrines they teach are but human precepts.* You drop what God commands and hold to human tradition. Yes, forsooth," he added, "you set aside what God commands, so as to maintain your own tradition! Thus, Moses said, *Honour your father and mother,* and *He who curses his father or mother is to suffer death.* But you say that if a man tells his father or mother, 'This money might have been at your service, but it is Korban' (that is, dedicated to God), he is exempt, so you hold, from doing anything for his father or mother. That is repealing the word of God in the interests of the tradition which you keep up. And you do many things like that."

Mark 7: 1-13 Moffatt

It was no doubt their conscience which drove them to crucify Jesus. It takes no stretch of the imagination to see that they actually felt better, were more cheerful, the day after Jesus was crucified. But their treatment of him was not very different from their treatment of others—publicans and sinners—of their day. Their conscience told them that, in destroying those who did not build up the kingdom as they conceived the building, they were serving God.

Notice their treatment of the woman taken in adultery, as recorded in John 8. The case was clear-cut. The woman was guilty. Their conscience was constructed on written rules given by Moses a long time before, rules that served a good purpose at one time. It was their duty to execute judgment. They would have felt guilty if they had been remiss in their duty. But was that all? No doubt this poor woman served a much more significant inner purpose for them. She was a kind of scapegoat for their own sins. She may have been an example by which they enforced the taboo against immorality—this, too, is a conscience maneuver, to try to lighten the personal strain by producing a more structured situation. Some of the Pharisees may have been acting out their own repressed sexuality by dealing with this woman's overt act. The gossips and the crusaders are often of this hard, deprived class.

In any case, Jesus came right to the heart of the conscience problem. He forced them to look at their own wash. Perhaps they were afraid he would hang it on the line for everybody to gaze at, just as they were treating this guilty woman. Such a procedure may not have produced mercy, but it certainly did bring their natural fears close to the surface.

This whole incident throws some light on how conscience operates. A primary component in conscience is fear of rejection. We, at first, take into ourselves—we "swallow"—the ideals and prohibitions of our parents and our neighbors. This "introjection," as the psychologists call it, occurs in order to keep us from being punished. That is, we learn that by internalizing these rules we control ourselves from within, and thereby avoid getting hurt—and we get rewarded too.

As we mature, the approved ways become ideals and sentiments which are a part of our real selves. But suppose we do not become identified with society. Suppose the ideals become merely the shrewd tricks by which we avoid punishment. Then we become hypocrites. Conscience, then, is what H. L. Mencken called it, "an inner voice that warns you that somebody is looking." We are good as a matter of expediency and bad when we think we can get by with it.

The Pharisees, like all human beings to some extent, were conscientious on some points (misguided in their case) and hypocrites on others. This shows clearly why conscience cannot be trusted under all circumstances. People have ways of rationalizing, some more than others. As Aldous Huxley says in *Eyeless in Gaza:* [3] "Men don't tell themselves that the wrong they are doing is wrong. Either they do it without thinking, or else they invent reasons for believing it's right."

The fact that the Pharisees wanted to destroy the woman and actually succeeded in crucifying Jesus illustrates another point. Someone has pointed out that most cultures destroy two groups, those who have too much conscience and those who have too little. Roger Williams is an example of the former, although not literally destroyed. And Sing Sing is full of the latter. Today we are prone to speak of the latter as having "character disorders." At least, many of them, because they cannot by conscience make themselves conform to the laws of God and man, are disorderly. Sometimes the more conscientious, the former group, are heroes or saints only after the world catches up with them. But both have a certain kind of upstairs resident.

THE APOSTLE PAUL'S CONSCIENCE

The apostle Paul is another instructive example of how the conscience operates. Hear him near the end of his ministry stand before the council in Jerusalem and say: "Men and brethren, I have lived in all good conscience before God until this day" (Acts 23: 1). Or hear him affirm to Governor Felix: "And herein do I exercise myself, to have always a conscience void of offence toward God, and toward men" (Acts 24: 16).

This was the Saul who "made havock of the church, entering into every house, and haling men and women committed them to prison." He held the clothes of those who stoned Stephen, the first Christian martyr. By all modern standards he was a murderer. He did to Christians what Communists have done to them in China. He "persecuted them even unto strange cities." All of this with a good conscience?

Later he explained to young Timothy that he "did it ignorantly in unbelief." Yes, but is there not some inner voice in every man that cries out against murder? Some would say, with J. A. Hadfield, that "conscience is the voice of repressed good." Where was the good in those destructive days in the life of Paul? If it was repressed, it was certainly also silent. Rather, it seems that the voice he heard was that of evil, urging him on to kill and imprison simple Christian witnesses.

No doubt if someone had said to Paul, "My dear brother, don't you know that there is in every human being an inner voice that tells him that he ought not injure or dominate his fellow man?" he would have answered: "A voice! A voice? You mean conscience? I want you to know that last night when I prayed my heart was relieved to feel that I was serving God with all my strength. I intend to stamp out this heresy. I could not live with myself if I did not."

This is very disturbing, but it need not be. We are forced to accept the conclusion that man may be fighting against God and still be cheerful in conscience. Or, a more common way, he may be ignoring God with no conscious pangs of conscience. The man upstairs is made what he is by the furnishings we put into his room. If they are good and true and beautiful, he will be the valuable help we need in forming our lives. If they are poor and shoddy and severe, our consciences may be like a frustrated old man, demanding, criticizing, unreasonable, and hateful.

Sabatini says of one of his characters, "He strangled his conscience that at best had never been robust." Paul speaks of such consciences. In the letter to Titus we read of those who have a "defiled conscience"—they seemed not to be able to distinguish between the pure and the impure (Titus 1: 15). In another place Paul describes people who seem insensible to right and wrong, "having their conscience seared with a hot iron" (1 Tim. 4: 2). He also writes of a "good conscience" (1 Tim. 3: 9). And the writer of Hebrews speaks of "purged" consciences. He apparently refers to those who had dispensed with the keeping of laws as a means of making themselves "feel good," like washing off the grime of a journey, to serving the living God (9: 14).

Asset or Liability?

There are several other passages which refer to the conscience but these may suffice. It seems clear that the human conscience may be both an asset and a liability. This is true for both the Christian and the non-Christian. And it has profound and demanding implications. Once a man realizes that he does not contain a kind of "divine outpost" which is trustworthy, he will be forced either to become thoroughly human or to sink to another level.

As I see it, an individual is forced to follow one or more of three paths. In the first place, he may conform to the group requirements—church, community, lodge, Communist cell, or even gang—and be as well satisfied as possible. In this case, he is following the other fellow's conscience. If the group is right, his way of life may be a fairly good one. He becomes a cog in the machine. He may be an idolater, but he may also be fairly comfortable. This is all some modern educators and sociologists seek.

On the other hand, he may furnish his upstairs with all sorts of queer, eccentric, and antisocial bric-a-brac. Conscience to him is simply one of the unfortunate parts of human evolution. He will repudiate it. All values are relative, including the "valuer," so he will follow his whim and his impulse. If the public does not like his way of life, the public be damned. Most of us have known such people. They are lost souls, unanchored ships, and houses with sand foundations. They have manipulated their consciences, but while they were doing it they divorced themselves from their fellows, who were the last possession on earth they wanted to lose.

THE GOOD CONSCIENCE

What, then, is the "conscience void of offence toward God and toward men" which Paul affirmed? Literally, such does not exist, nor ever did, if he means that he behaved in such a manner that others were not offended by him. There is no such sublime state on this planet. Paul even discovered that he had been persecuting the lowly Nazarene himself. He gave Peter a very embarrassing time at Antioch (Gal. 2:11). And nearly everywhere he went he ended up in a riot or a revival.

This very situation leads us to point out that conscience consists of much more than knowledge of right and wrong.

It is primarily a "prompter" or a will-to-action. As T. V. Smith has said, "Conscience is the penalty we pay for being active creatures in a world of manifold possibilities of action." When a man says "I ought to do this instead of that," he may be said to be acting in a "conscience manner." If he lies awake all night and moans, "Oh, why did I do it, why did I do it?" his conscience is working but not in its highest function. It should have served to foresee and warn rather than merely to remember and punish.

There are really some critical problems which are at the heart of our human existence. The first one is: How do I know the right way? The second is: Should I feel guilty over this failure? If so, how guilty am I? If not, how shall I take the edge off the sharp sword of punishment? A third one is: After knowing the right way, how do I find the inclination to do it? It is equivalent to saying that the man upstairs needs a brain, a backbone, and a heart. If any one of these is weak, we may be tyrannized by our conscience or anesthetized by it. Either equals failure to be our best.

The Christian view of these problems centers around Christ. A conscience does not become healthy by reading rules about positive thinking. Affirmations are but a form of autohypnosis. Is that what the mature Christian seeks?

CULTIVATING THE CONSCIENCE

It would seem that the sensible solution to our conscience problems lies in two directions.

First, the conscience *needs educating*. A good conscience is one which speaks up to warn, to tell the truth about duty, and to hurt only in proportion to the failure to do God's will. We are not a law unto ourselves, as Paul described the heathen pattern (Rom. 2:14-15). We were made to be responsible subjects. But nothing will take the place of our searching for moral truth. Jesus questioned in his day, "Why even of yourselves judge ye not what is right?" (Luke 12:57). And Paul states boldly, "Let every man be fully persuaded in his own mind" (Rom. 14:5).

This training of the conscience is a constant process. The conscience must be kept in trim. A revision of ideals and a revamping of habit patterns is as important for the conscience as the training of a vine that grows on a trellis. Often we need to get on our knees. Not infrequently we need a ladder to reach toward heaven. But one thing is certain, we need to take our consciences firmly in hand and make them serve the ends of our best understanding.

Finally, a good conscience *must be obeyed*. Many people never get any nearer obedience than a bad conscience—they feel bad but they never get around to doing good. "I knew I ought to but I just didn't get to it," we say. "To obey is better than sacrifice" might be paraphrased to read "To act is better than to regret." It does not matter how well we explain away our sense of responsibility; unless we do what we know to be right we twist our consciences and impair our capacity for moral behavior. Coleridge expressed this idea in "Fears in Solitude":

> For never true courage dwells with them,
> Who, playing tricks with conscience, dare not look
> At their own vices.

To quote Professor Smith again, "Conscience must be made to face its cross, for the sake of man and his future." And T. S. Eliot has written that "your business is not to clear your conscience but to learn how to bear the burden on your conscience."

It is when conscience faces its cross that it grows. This is another way of saying that there is no growth without anxiety or pain. Guilt feelings are painful. To be dissatisfied with ourselves is not an easy state. But unless a Christian is willing to say "I have sinned," he may not expect to move out of a state of lethargy. "God be merciful to me a sinner" need not overwhelm one with a sense of inadequacy.

It is here that Christ and his revelation of the Father can be of tremendous help to us. His mercy in accepting us in our present state of development is counterbalanced by his call, "Follow thou me." Then, conscience becomes more than an inside consciousness of what society demands, and it issues into a normal response of the creature to the Creator. Now, the conscience does not tyrannize us by causing us to writhe in pain over past failures. These are forgiven. Nor does it rest from its labors as if we have outgrown responsibility or are taking a moral holiday. We are always "before God."

There is a story about Phidias working on the statue of Athene for the Acropolis at Athens. He was perfecting her hair, bringing out with the keen edge of his chisel every line and filament. A passerby said, "What is the use of such painstaking with that part of the work? That statue is to go up a hundred feet high, and the back of the head will be toward the wall and nobody will see it." To this criticism Phidias replied simply, "The gods will see it."

TAPROOTS FOR TALL SOULS 5

THE Japanese for centuries have cultivated an art which has amazed sightseers. It is called Bonsai. It is the practice of taking tall trees—regular yard or forest variety—and dwarfing them. It is largely the art of aristocrats, because ordinary laborers do not have the required time. It is a very tedious process, consisting of careful watering, nipping the buds, thinning the roots, fertilizing, and containing the roots within a given space. It is an old art that goes back, at least, to the thirteenth century. These potted trees, looking in every respect like the full size ones of the same species, are an amazing wonder. At present, in our country, many people are acquiring the art, as indicated by the advertisements of "Miniature Tree Kits" that are running in our better magazines.

There is a widespread myth in the Western world that the Bonsai trick is that of tying up or clipping the taproots. Though entirely in error, it serves as a good illustration of spiritual dwarfing. Everyone who has lived on the farm knows the value of a taproot to a plant. Surface roots are good; but a principal root, going deep into the earth, is important, too. Sometimes a farmer throws away plants, which he is transplanting, if they have no taproots.

Quite a different extreme in tree growth are the giant Sequoias of California. They are not the tallest in the world; the eucalyptus of Australia have that honor. But they are the most massive, weighing nearly 1,000 tons. One of the redwoods grows to a height of 364 feet.

The most noted of all the redwoods is known as "General Sherman Tree" in the Sequoia National Park. It is 101½ feet in circumference, 32 feet in diameter at the base, 27 feet in diameter at 8 feet above ground, 18½ feet at 100 feet above base, and it is 282 feet tall. It is reputed to be the largest tree in the world and the oldest living thing, probably being between two and three thousand years old.

What roots it must take to hold erect such giant trees in the storm! There are some trees, not redwoods, I have been told, whose taproot goes down into the ground as far as the top extends above. Be that as it may, it takes deep and strong roots to make tall trees stand up and keep growing.

Christians Should Grow Tall

These two kinds of trees may serve as parables of our spiritual lives. The potted-plant tree must have its matted roots clipped at times to keep it dwarfed. The giant redwood sends its roots deep into mountain soil. What are the factors which control the growth of a Christian? Someone may say that the answer is obvious: the main factor in growing a tall tree is to have a tall species. But Christians are supposed to grow tall. We are the giant species. No one can read the New Testament and suppose that we are to be the potted-plant variety.

The fact is, that without Jesus Christ as our standard the world lacks a measuring rod for human growth. How are we to decide when we are mature? When is a person full grown spiritually? Are we to take Socrates, Francis of Assisi, or

Abraham Lincoln as our standard? Or is there no goal except that of self-realization? It is a fact that, so far as I can see, has gone quite unnoticed, that modern thinkers who reject or neglect the New Testament do not know how tall, spiritually and emotionally, a man may grow. Without Christ, we have no model as well as no life. He is the only fully grown man who ever walked this earth. All of us are somewhere between infancy and Christ.

Let us come back to a passage mentioned in chapter I. Here are excerpts from Dr. W. O. Carver's paraphrase of Ephesians 4: 11-16 which gives its real meaning:

> The objective which the ascended Lord in all these creative functions in his Church is *facing* is *the perfecting of the saints in related unity for and in the work of service,* with *the* great *end in view of the building up of the Body of the Christ. . . .* This purpose is nothing short of our attaining *unto mature man*hood, yes even *unto the measure of the stature of the fully developed Christ. . . .*
>
> *. . . We shall no longer* be content to remain *babes,* lacking in responsibility, understanding, and intelligent self-direction toward our goal, mere *tossing waves and carried around* here and there without aim or order *by every* chance *wind of teaching.*

Paul sets forth here both sides of the growth situation, our immaturity and the mature standard, Christ. On the debit side of the ledger there is instability, irresponsibility, refusal to think and act for self. Paul pictures an individual who is only half an individual, directed by the forces around him rather than making decisions himself. It is what modern anthropologists call "other-directed" rather than "inner-directed."

Over against this pattern of behavior stands the Christ. He is the "fully developed" one and is our goal of mature manhood. He was not simply an individualist, for what is called individualism is usually self-worship and adolescence. Christ was mature enough to say, "I came down from heaven, not to do mine own will, but the will of him that sent me" (John 6: 38). This alone is spiritual maturity. If he had been human only, he would have said, "I came to serve my fellowman." That sounds like a worthy goal, but it is really a projected self-worship. It is an inverted egoism. We see ourselves in our fellows, and, therefore, out of selfishness (although hardly conscious of what we are doing) we glorify them.

In the epistle to the Romans also, Paul presents Christ as our goal. He gathers up the whole purpose of God in sending Christ to save the world in the words, that we might "be conformed to the image of his Son, that he might be the firstborn among many brethren" (8:29). It is plain that Christians are expected to be different from their former selves. Christlike is perhaps as good a word as any. We are to be "Christs," with the same characteristics and purposes, of the same family.

This involves growth toward Christlikeness, not only in morals but in the whole complex personality of Christ. It applies to disposition, temperament, spiritual attitudes, faith, and mental health. It affects such traits as humility, courage, sincerity, sacrifice, respect for others, and many others. These are only some of the ways in which we are to be like him.

We ask, "How, then, does the soul grow; how do we grow tall like Christ?"

> How does the soul grow? Not all in a minute;
> Now it may lose ground, and now it may win it;
> Now it resolves, and again the will faileth;
> Now it rejoiceth, and now it bewaileth;
> Now its hopes fructify, then they are blighted;
> Now it walks sullenly, now gropes benighted;
> Fed by discouragements, taught by disaster;
> So it goes forward, now slower, now faster,
> Till all the pain is past, and failure made whole,
> It is full grown, and the Lord rules the soul.
>
> SUSAN COOLIDGE

It seems to me that the words of Jesus, as recorded in John 15, attempt to answer this very question. He is talking to the apostles, to the inner circle, to the very people who would have needed this least, it would seem. We may judge, then, that Jesus considered the ideas presented here of tremendous importance.

THE VINE AND THE BRANCHES

Jesus said that our relationship to him is like that of a branch to the main stem or body of a grapevine. If the branch does not bear fruit, it will be cut off and burned. This applies to Christians who will not be blessed of God if they do not bear fruit. Jesus was talking about this life, not hereafter. He suggested that a pruning or cleansing has already taken place in their lives (John 15:3), so now it is his concern that they learn to stay clean. Then he states two clear principles:

1. "Without me ye can do nothing" (v. 5). He does not say that by ourselves we will be handicapped, or inferior, or not quite our best. He says that we will be complete failures. We are as constantly dependent on Christ as the branch is dependent on the vine. Even as a branch begins to wither within a few minutes after it is cut from the vine, so we are dependent on Christ.

That is a great lesson for modern Christianity. We are apt to depend on organization, education, or even on preaching. Especially do we lean toward organization. Some modern churchmen seem to think that a great world church organization, eliminating sects and divisions, would bring in the millennium. Rather, we should remember that if Christ is to win in this highly competitive world, it will be due to Christ himself, not to his church, or even to his teachings, apart from himself. The living Christ alone can sustain living Christians.

2. "Continue to live in me"—this is literally what Jesus said. Such a life is the opposite of self-sufficiency. And since he commands it, we may be sure that it is a conscious process. We may well suppose that grapevines grow without anything like consciousness, yet no one can explain the inner process of plant life. But to "continue in me" is certainly, for Christains, a way of life that involves awareness. We must not only be aware of Christ's help, but it is necessary to be aware of our awareness to maintain our personal fellowship with him.

There are four aspects of this continuing to live in Christ. The first one is obvious: we must admit to ourselves our dependence on him. Second, his words must continue in us (v. 7). Earlier, Jesus had said that if a man loves him, he will "keep" his words. Third, we must be obedient. "If ye keep my commandments, ye shall abide in my love" (v. 10). Fourth, we should pray effectively. "If ye abide in me and my words abide in you, ye shall ask what ye will, and it shall be done unto you" (v. 7). The successful prayer, according to this, grows out of a heart absorbed in the words of Christ and conscious of the presence of Christ.

Usually we overlook another clause in this passage, which may indeed be the most important one. "Continue ye in my love" (v. 9). Jesus pours into this all of the divine love, saying that he loves us as the Father loved him. Now live in my love, he says. Depend upon it. Remain inside it just as you are surrounded by the thick, brick wall in the winter. Browning said, "God, Thou art love; I build my life on that." Sidney Lanier had the same idea in "The Marshes of Glynn."

> As the marsh-hen secretly builds on the watery sod,
> Behold I will build me a nest on the greatness of God:
> I will fly in the greatness of God as the marsh-hen flies
> In the freedom that fills all the space 'twixt the marsh and
>   the skies:

By so many roots as the marsh-grass sends in the sod
I will heartily lay me a-hold on the greatness of God.

THE PARABLE OF THE SOILS

Jesus used another illustration of growth, somewhat similar
to the vine and branches, in his parable of the soils or, as it is
sometimes called, the sower. Some seed fell on the hard, beaten
paths across the field. The birds came and ate it. Other seed
fell on shallow soil and was quickly withered by the heat because it had no deep roots. Others fell among thorns and were
soon choked. But the good ground which brought forth an
hundredfold represents, Jesus said, individuals who have "an
honest and good heart" (Luke 8: 15).

Christianity is a religion which emphasizes the inwardness
of all behavior. We might well call it a heart religion, in con-
trast with a morality religion or a ritualistic religion. Jesus
internalized morality and religious behavior. If our acts do
not come from the heart they can never be good acts. To be
honest, to perform cold acts of kindness or self-denial, these
may be good up to a point, but they are not Christian. "Thou
desirest truth in the inward parts" is a great summary statement from the psalms. "Blessed are the pure in heart."

L. H. Marshall of Canada has said, "Many a humble and un-
lettered disciple of Christ has gained a moral insight and understanding which excels that of Plato or Aristotle or any other
moral philosopher." The very taproot of spiritual growth is "a
good and honest heart," one that is open to the Word and is
not shut off from God by worldly affairs. "No heart is pure
that is not passionate, no virtue is safe that is not enthusiastic."

Jesus said that these good and honest hearts, having heard
the word, "keep it, and bring forth fruit with patience" (Luke
8: 15). This reminds us of Luke's account of the Bereans

when Paul visited their city: "These were more noble than
those in Thessalonica, in that they received the word with all
readiness of mind, and searched the scriptures daily, whether
those things were so" (Acts 17: 11). It seems that the response
to the Word of God reveals two important facts about an individual: whether he may be expected to grow and the present
condition of his heart.

I do not know what a good and honest heart means to
others, but to me it means sincerity and seriousness. It may be
granted that there is a kind of sincerity which is naive and
refuses to grow up. Some religions are like that. Such are those
who accept uncritically what "the church" or "the traditions"
prescribe. But there is also a kind of sincerity which is fair
and open-minded and is seriously concerned for the good and
the true.

The longer I live the more I think of intelligent sincerity as
one of the important roots of great souls. All of us have heard
someone say patronizingly, "Oh, so-and-so is sincere, I suppose; he seems awfully simple to me, but I guess he is sincere."
When you have said "He is sincere," you have said perhaps
the best thing that can be said about a Christian. To be thoroughly sincere is rare and most commendable.

Rooted in Love

There is one other passage which deals with spiritual roots
for tall souls. It is a phrase Paul uses in his letter to the Ephesians: "rooted and grounded in love." The context is a prayer
for the Ephesian Christians. It is a beautiful and comprehensive prayer. It goes as deep as the human heart and as high and
wide as the love of God. The very heart of it is the phrase
quoted above. Paul's idea seems to be that unless we are spiritually rooted in love we cannot grow tall in our understanding

of God—"to know the love of Christ, which passeth knowledge, that ye might be filled with all the fulness of God" (Eph. 3: 19).

Love is a method of learning. We cannot learn the love of God by hearing a lecture on it or by being told that we ought to love. We learn love by being loved. Normally, we become rooted and grounded in it in our childhood. But this is often impaired by the kind of love we received in childhood. God's love is boundless and free. Human love is conditional and limited. Most people have to overcome the errors of their parents, and the consequent deformities of their own personalities, by becoming rooted in the love of God. We can no more grow without this deep rootage than a tree can grow in mid-air.

All of us are thinking in these days how we can plant the trees of peace in a forest so torn by strife. Our world needs to be rooted and grounded in love. At present, we are afflicted with the small-scale individual in places of leadership which demand giants. John Foster Dulles has stated our situation very clearly:

The great lack of the world today is that there are too few Christians, and when I say Christians I do not mean those who seek ecclesiastical marriage and burial and who occasionally contribute to church support. I speak of the number of those who actually possess the spiritual qualities Christ taught and who realize such qualities are designed for practical use.

Summarizing the revelation of God on the subject of rootage for growth, fundamental concepts are presented at various places in the New Testament: (1) our utter and constant dependence on Christ; (2) the necessity of conscious living in Christ; (3) sincerity in receiving the word of Christ; and (4) diligence in expressing daily our love for Christ. These are roots that support tall souls.

How Tall Shall We Grow?

An important thread of thought running through all of these passages is that our goal and aim is to grow toward the height of Christ. God is in the process of growing tall souls. May he pity us if we do not aim at the same kind of strong, tall souls.

Bishop McDowell told Dr. William L. Stidger about a boy he knew in college, whom we shall call Jones. Jones was the outstanding student, orator, athlete, personality in a certain college, and everybody expected him to turn the world upside down. He seemed to have the brightest future of any of the students. A quarter of a century later Bishop McDowell met a woman graduate of that college, and they talked over old times and old friends. Finally, Bishop McDowell said, "And what happened to Jones? We thought he would be in the United States Senate by now. And yet he has dropped out of sight as completely as if the sea had swallowed him up. What has happened to him?"

"Why, don't you know, Bishop, what happened to Jones?"

"No, what happened to him?"

"Why, Jones caught up with his own horizons, Bishop."

That happened to Cain, Esau, Samson, Saul, David at one time, the apostle Paul before the Damascus Road experience, and the church of the Laodiceans. It is happening all of the time. We end up as dwarfs when we were made to be Sequoias.

> What is left for us, save, in growth
> Of soul, to rise up, far past both,
> From the gift looking to the giver,
> And from the cistern to the river,
> And from the finite to infinity,
> And from man's dust to God's divinity?
>
> ROBERT BROWNING

LEARNING TO MANAGE MYSELF 6

I AM my world's number one problem. All of the "problems" of mankind have arisen because individuals like myself could not manage themselves. Of course, it would be more flattering to me if I could say that the problem people of the world are not in my class; they are across the tracks or out in the country or members of another religious faith. But such is not the case. Even if I had managed myself well up to this present moment—which I haven't—there is nothing to keep me from becoming a failure an hour from now.

The Bible puts this matter plainly. "So the man who thinks he stands securely must be on the lookout not to fall" (1 Cor. 10:12 Williams). "Brothers, if anybody is caught in the very act of doing wrong, you who are spiritual, in the spirit of gentleness, must set him right; each of you continuing to think of yourself, for you may be tempted too" (Gal. 6:1 Williams). Or the words of the Master himself ought to stab us wide awake: "You must all keep watching and praying that you may not be exposed to temptation. Man's spirit is willing but human nature is weak" (Matt. 26:41 Williams).

One of the most remarkable aspects of the Bible is its honest facing of human failure and weakness.

I Am My Problem

Somewhere there is a line of poetry which says, "When the rose decks herself, she adorns the garden!" My obligation to be an attractive, stable, worthwhile Christian is certainly a primary one. I may work hard in the church or in the community; I may provide well for my family; I may produce so far as service is concerned—but if I am not the kind of person who is a good example of my religion, I am missing my greatest opportunity. Is that not the meaning of 1 Corinthians 13?

It is simpler in the case of the rose. It grows automatically, so far as we human beings know. In our case, life will not stand still. We never step into the same stream twice, as the ancients put it. Life changes. We change. Even after we get right we have the problem of staying right. Today, I may be comparatively poised, happy, and useful. Tomorrow, I may be overwhelmed by tragedy, may be whimpering and dejected. There are mood swings within and weather conditions, wars, and economic depressions without. There is tremendous social pressure, conscious and unconscious, that envelops us on the one hand; there are wild, irrational, biological and egocentric drives which arise from within, on the other.

Sometimes we hanker for a social group which will control us (although we never quite put it in these words); some stable, non-threatening, directing institution or social setting where we will not have so many conflicts and so many decisions to make. Instead our world is in a state of flux. Rural and town young people go away to college and to war. City people, young and old, are living next door to people they do not know or, if they do, they do not like. On religion, social customs, morals and education we do not agree, and we do not feel close to one another. We need more of a sense of belong-

ing, but, at present and in the near future, it is very unlikely
that we can depend on that personal support.

Dr. Lewis J. Sherrill of Union Seminary in New York has
put it this way:[1] "Modern civilization requires that the individual be a person of extraordinary strength if he is to thrive
in the midst of that civilization ... And yet, on the other hand,
modern society is producing, in vast numbers, persons who are
rendered deficient because they cannot achieve precisely that
kind of strength and maturity which our civilization demands."

PAUL'S VIEW

The apostle Paul faces the problem of self-management,
even after years of Christian work: "Any man who enters an
athletic contest practices rigid self-control in training, only to
win a wreath that withers, but we are in to win a wreath that
never withers. So that is the way I run, with no uncertainty
as to winning. That is the way I box, not like one that punches
the air. But I keep on beating and bruising my body and making it my slave, so that I, after I have summoned others to the
race, may not myself become unfit to run" (1 Cor. 9:25-27
Williams).

This vivid and bold figure is taken from the great athletic
festivals of the day. To excel—to win the cup, in modern
parlance—was the height of ambition for man. Paul's goal was
Christlike character and the reward of a life spent for Christ.
So he declares the strenuousness of this character-task. (See
also Rom. 8:13; 1 Cor. 4:11 f.; 2 Cor. 4:7 f.; Col. 3:5; 1 Peter
4:1.) Like athletic exercises, it requires discipline. Paul was a
spiritual pugilist, as every Christian worth the name must be.

He was not interested in shadow-boxing. That is the practice of those who are unskilled in the ring and, in religious

life, corresponds to the self-punishing fasts and self-denials that are prescribed. Many people waste good energy trying to get themselves in shape to live the Christian life. They are told that fasting will serve as an antidote for fast living. At Easter they leave off tobacco or alcoholic beverages or certain foods. It seems never to occur to them to question, "Is there a carry-over? Is there, to put it in modern language, any transfer of training?" Some of us have experimented with fasting and found it wanting. No "beating the air" is needed in following Christ. Real discipline consists of decisions to say "Yes" to Christ and "No" to self, in everyday situations.

Let us not underestimate the importance of decisions, of responsibility. The Christian way is often rocky and uphill. That is why the inspired Paul says, literally, "I beat my body black and blue and make a slave of it." Climbing the heights, weighted down by heavy baggage, is often necessary. Christianity is no "cosmic escalator," as Rufus Jones has put it. But we must struggle

> Upon the great world's *altar stairs*
> That slope through darkness up to God.

Growing souls do not ask, "Do I like to do this task? Does it contribute to my happiness?" They doggedly put one foot in front of the other and do their duty.

Perhaps at this point we should observe some of the ways we fail. Paul was concerned that after he had preached he might do a poor job of practicing. He might be "a castaway," or rejected for the prize or reward. All of us have seen people like that. Esau, Moses at Nebo, Samson, Achan, Saul, Judas, Demas, in the Bible. In my first pastorate a man in his fifties told me how much he would like to work in the church. "But," said he, "my record is such in the community that I am afraid I will do more harm than good; people do not trust me." He was a fine man, though with some "blots on the 'scutcheon." Later he committed suicide. Unfortunately, I was not able to recognize his reaction as depression. His failure was first within himself.

FOUR WAYS TO FAIL

We have special phrases in our language which describe the loss of self-control. We say, "He may blow up." A person may be going along doing his job fairly smoothly, in the home, at work, or in church. Suddenly, he flies off the handle, he explodes, he slashes out at someone, he blows up. Someone gets a tongue lashing. He may try to justify it by saying that it is better to express anger than to repress it, or make some similar excuse. He seems never to have heard the counsel of Proverbs: "He that is slow to anger is better than the mighty; and he that ruleth his spirit than he that taketh a city."

Another expression which describes personal failure is "fold up." When the emotional load gets heavy, he just gives up. The straw which breaks the camel's back may be a disappointment in love, a quarrel with a friend, a divorce, the loss of a job, or even a misunderstanding at church. Nothing shows our immaturity quite as clearly as frustration.

Mary was a little handicapped by her short stature. She was married, had a beautiful child, and everything seemed to be going fine. But her husband was not doing well at his job. He had been very quarrelsome lately. Added to this Mary had some surgery and was seriously ill for a few weeks. Then came the critical blow. She found evidence that he was "stepping out." What was she to do? Her husband admitted the failure and promised to behave himself in the future. But Mary's pride could not take the blow. She "folded up" and went back to her mother. A divorce followed.

A similar reaction is described by the expression, "He went off the deep end." It applies to being overcome by temptation. A man becomes involved in financial needs and "goes off the deep end" by writing cold checks or using money for himself which is not his. A woman is in love with some attractive male who is not worthy of her devotion. She refuses to recognize this and is later disappointed and becomes bitter. A man "goes off the deep end" in drink or gambling or even in his enthusiasm for some false ideology. Then, after an extended spree, it becomes much harder to rebuild his life.

A fourth form of failure is less dramatically expressed but far more frequent and more dangerous: "drifting." Someone has said, "There are a few people who make things happen, the many people who watch things happen, and the overwhelming majority who have no notion of what happens." I saw the terrifying danger of this last attitude once when, in a rowboat, fishing; I almost drifted into a very powerful whirlpool. Dreaming through life does not always deal with us so excitingly. Usually, we just dawdle our time away, or we rush from one trifle to another, trying to satisfy demands which are as contradictory as lust and chastity.

Such a "drifter" came to me about eight months after he and his wife had obtained a divorce. He had been a rather good church worker until the marital trouble. Gradually he had withdrawn from his friends. He was working regularly but seemed to have lost interest. Ambition seemed to have become a weak, pointless, experience. He said to me, "I'm just spinning my wheels. My drive is gone. At one time I had great hopes for the future. Now I don't have either hopes or fears. I'm just drifting."

Of course, the people who blow up, fold up, go off the deep end, or drift, do not constitute all of the types of failures. And these experiences do not constitute the whole of life. But they are examples of not being able to manage ourselves. Who has not over-reacted to some seeming injury? And who has lived long without going through a period of marking time? The important question, it seems, is what to do when we realize that the brakes do not work or the clutch is slipping? Are we to be fatalistic and say that "what is to be will be"? Is just giving-in the answer? Or, on the other hand, is the secret to "thank whatever gods may be for my unconquerable soul"? Not to wince or cry aloud is not enough. We may ache inside and finally blow our brains out.

Ego Strength

The psychologist speaks of this ability to function well under strain and stress as "ego strength." He means the ability a person has within himself to face the hard facts of reality and to accept them. A weak ego has to develop ways of avoiding reality. Sometimes, it is simply shrinking from conflict. Again, it may be a complete departure from reality: one may hear voices or imagine that he is Napoleon or God. A strong ego accepts responsibility, makes constructive moves, produces the good life, and grows toward a more mature self. The ego strength is what the general public means by "will power."

Here we come face to face with the fact that only God knows how responsible a person is. This is particularly important when we try to help other people. It is easy for a wife to say to a husband, "Now, I know you can do better than that." Or for a husband to say, "All of that complaining is silly. You just think you are sick. Snap out of it and quit worrying about yourself." Quit worrying! Was ever a piece of advice more useless? All that it does usually is to add to the person's guilt-feelings and thereby increases his fears that he is inadequate. A much better method, if a husband or wife wants to be helpful, would be to say, "I love you, and I hope that you can find the forces within you to overcome this; but I will continue to love you anyway."

In this day when emotional illnesses are so prevalent the question of how to strengthen our "ego controls" is a primary one. We need all of the help we can obtain. Christianity has been working at the task of making people strong for 2000 years. The Master himself left people clothed and in their right minds. Paul wrote, "Be strong in the Lord and in the power of his might." He likened the equipment for Christian living to a Roman soldier's armor (see Eph. 6: 10-17). One of his most striking phrases, "having done all, to stand," states the aim of the life of faith; when people do what they can to change the world and then stand firm at their posts, they grow inside, and God works through them.

Perhaps, however, some suggestions about how to be "strong in the Lord" may be in order. When we are weak, how do we go about strengthening ourselves? How do we grow in self-management?

CHECK YOUR LOVE LIFE

A good place to start is in personal inventory. *Check up on your love life.* It is no accident that "Thou shalt love the Lord thy God" is the first commandment. When a person has a deep love for God he is constantly strengthened by it. It removes unnecessary fears. "Perfect love casteth out fear."

A missionary in Africa says that most of the people with whom she works are filled with fears. They are afraid of all kinds of spirits, of a world of magic and superstition. But, says the missionary, we teach them that behind all these seemingly dangerous objects is a great loving Father who controls all and is always good.

How do people learn love? Not merely by having a lesson on it. Not by self-discipline. We do not tighten our belts, stick out our chins and say, "Now I'm going to love God, if it kills me." No, we learn to love by first being loved and then responding to it. Only then can it be effective in our lives and reach its fulfilment. Even God's love will mean nothing to us unless we accept it. His love gets through to us only when we recognize and respond to it. Then, as we come to understand and experience his great, eternal, sacrificial love for us, we learn to love him more deeply and our fellow man more unselfishly. The whole life and message of Christ was God's great revelation of his love for us. But those who refuse Christ will never experience it, so they cannot build a deep, emotional life. We must build on the fact of God's revealed love, or we build on sand.

Then, we must let God love others through us. Only the love of God can make us go straight. If we refuse to allow that love to become the controlling force in our lives there is no hope to keep us from "acting out" our wild impulses.

There is a type of emotional disorder which many psychiatrists call "psychopathic." They also speak of the victims as being "psychopathic deviates," "constitutional psychopaths" or as having—and this is the more recent terminology —"character disorders." Such persons are not insane and not simply nervous, often not nervous at all. They merely "act out" their impulses. They write cold checks, lie, drink, use dope, and violate other moral codes. They are unstable and nonconforming. But the significant thing about every one of them is that they do not form any deep emotional attachments. They may outwardly show affection or friendliness, but they lack deep loyalties and identification with other people, which would afford stability.

A mother and father brought a nineteen year old boy to me.

He had been writing cold checks and was doing a number of other things which were getting him in trouble. They had reared him, as best they knew, to be a good boy; but, for some reason, his loyalties did not run deep enough. No amount of persuasion seemed to help him. I said to him, "Do you ever feel sorry for what you have done and confess your sins to God?" The manner of his answer struck me. In a bright, cheerful, almost flippant voice he replied, "O yeah." I thought to myself, a man who really loves people and feels deeply about his sins does not answer so merrily. Finally, I had to tell his parents that the only hope for him was in deep psychological therapy, which was probably impossible outside of some institution.

The fact is, however, that all of us have some of this "acting out" trouble. Laziness is one form. Anger, dishonesty, and any other antisocial behavior patterns are all in this class. The cure for those of us who are not seriously impaired—in which case, the help of a specialist is needed—is to deepen our emotional attachments. Any other approach is symptom treatment only; we need to deal with the cause. Love is the real treatment. We need to love God and to love our fellows with pure, unbreakable, all-giving, and all-forgiving love. To grow in this kind of love is an obvious need for all of us, and a possibility.

Admit Character Defects

A second approach to self-management is this: *We must admit our character defects.* Preachers and teachers may hold up high standards of good behaviour, but mental assent to these is not enough. We must face ourselves and say, "Thou ailest there and there and there."

Too often we think of sin as event, while actually it is always a personal act or decision. Some people think that confession of sin means to recount the episodes in which we did wrong and admit that we were there, even involved. I doubt that rehearsing our failures in confession of our sins to God does us any good or pleases God. It seems to me that true confession involves more than that. We need to ask ourselves, "Why did I tell that lie or fall into that habit or refuse that job that I was asked to do? What is wrong with my character that I have failed in that respect?"

This is involved in what the New Testament means by repentance and cross-bearing. In repentance, a person gets a new mind about his conduct. He not only sees that he committed a wrong act, but he admits that the reason he did it was because he had the wrong attitude toward God. That is why the Bible speaks of "repentance toward God." And when Jesus said, "If any man will come after me . . . let him take up his cross daily," he was calling us to accept the hard aspects of life. Crosses are to die on. As we accept the frustration of resisting temptation, we die to infantilism and become adult.

It takes courage to face our real defects and to ask God to change us. We know that in the very act of prayer we must accept responsibility for making right decisions. We must cooperate with God if he is to help us. Sometimes this means accepting and living with anxiety. There is no escaping conflict. In other words, we cannot save our faces and save our souls (or grow spiritually) at the same time.

LIVE IN THE PRESENT

A third force in strengthening our skill at self-direction is to *learn to act in the present.*

Everyone has met the elderly person who is turning all his thoughts back to childhood: "When I was a boy, etc." "I remember just as well as if it was yesterday the time when . . ." and then a long harangue about "the good old days." No one wishes to be unkind to those for whom memories of childhood events have become so vivid, but living in the past is a poor tonic for spiritual growth. It is a way of rubbing yourself in on yourself, and those about you are not very interested in the process.

On the other hand, many young people and some others are eternal dreamers. Tomorrow they will pray more, become great Christians, do the heroic deed, make a reputation. But today they fail to study, neglect to read, use only half of their brain-power. They do not realize that people who wake up to find themselves famous or successful or great saints usually haven't been asleep. All of us are like Scarlett O'Hara in *Gone with the Wind* when she said, "I won't think about that today. I'll do something about it tomorrow."

Of course, human beings cannot blot out their memories, any more than they can refrain from fearing the future at times. But we can grab the reins of our minds and say, "Whoa, I have today on my hands now; my present obligation is to live it well." Sir William Osler, the great Christian physician, used to talk about living in "day-tight compartments." He said that we need to undress our souls at night like we do our bodies. Alcoholics Anonymous members talk about beginning the day by praying to God and saying, "I may drink the rest of my life; I cannot promise; but today, help me to stay completely free of drink this day." Then, at the close of the day, they thank him for victory.

This is what great Christians have always done. They live in a state of constant responsibility. Others may take time out, declare moral holidays, make exceptions, but we know that to do so is to turn our backs upon God and to regress. God must work through us. But he does so as we acknowledge at any given time that we are "under God" and must depend upon his help.

Just before Jesus went back to the Father, Peter pointed to John and said, "Master, what about this man? What do you want him to do?" Jesus was almost severe when he answered, in effect, "If it is my will that he stay on this earth until I come again, what is that to you? You follow me for yourself!" (John 21:20-23). It is the old story of thinking of finding God's will in a long-range life program. What he says to us is that if we would find His will it must be in the proper management of our lives one day at a time.

GROWTH IN GETTING 7
ALONG WITH PEOPLE

EVERY man is a problem in search of a solution. We are born into a world that is autocratic. That is, from the very first we are pushed around, given orders, bossed, made to conform. And the child's problem is to learn how to move from an autocratic world to a democratic one. We must learn how to boss ourselves instead of being bossed—and it is a slow, painful process. Children grow only as they learn how to solve problems which are gradually pitched into their laps.

Learning to get along with people is one problem with which every one of us must deal. It is certainly necessary to happiness, usefulness, and success. It is even necessary to survival. Many of us remember the words of Franklin Delano Roosevelt's 1945 Jefferson Day speech which he did not live to deliver: "Today we are faced with the pre-eminent fact that if civilization is to survive, we must cultivate the science of human relationships—the ability of all peoples, of all kinds, to live together and work together in the same world at peace." [1] Whether we agree with the word "science" or not, we certainly agree that we must learn to live together.